It's All in the Soil

By Barbara Gannett

Contents

Earth's Soil

Soil is made up of tiny pieces of rock. It also contains bits of dead plants and animals that have **decayed**, or broken down. Millions of living things, such as **bacteria** and **fungi**, are also part of the soil. People depend on soil for farming and food. It holds heat, water and food for plants.

Many plants live in soil.

Try It Out

What's in the Soil?

- Take a handful of soil from the ground.

- Spread the soil out on paper.

- Look at the soil with a magnifying glass.

- What can you see? Roots? Dead leaves? Pebbles? Insects? Twigs?

- List what you find.

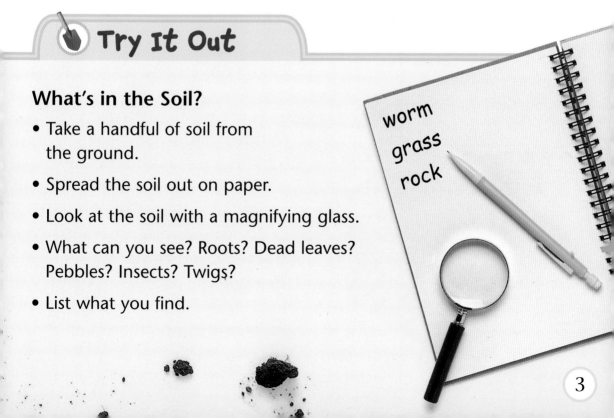

worm
grass
rock

How Soil Forms

Soil forms slowly over thousands of years.
Most soil is a mixture of four different materials:
humus (HYEW-muhs), rocks, water and air.
Humus is made up of decaying plants and animals.

Bits of broken rocks make up most of soil.
Rocks are broken into smaller pieces by a process
called **weathering**. Water and air fill up the
spaces between the pieces of rock and humus.

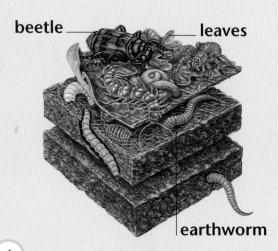

beetle —— leaves

earthworm

What Is Humus?

Tiny creatures live in the top
part of soil. There are also pieces
of rotting leaves and other dead
plants and animals. Over time,
bacteria and **fungi** will help
decay these once-living things
into humus. Humus has most
of the **nutrients** that plants
need to grow.

Erosion of fields along the banks of the River Severn, in Gloucestershire.

Wind and rain can carry soil to different places. This is called **erosion**. This can harm farmland and **pollute** rivers and streams.

Sometimes erosion happens very quickly. If there are no trees or grasses, soil can be washed or blown away very easily. If there are trees and grasses, their roots hold the soil in place.

Soil Layers

Soil forms in many different layers. First is the **topsoil**. It is made up of the smallest grains. It usually contains lots of **humus** and **nutrients**. Most plant roots are found here.

Next is the **subsoil**. It is made up of larger grains. It contains less humus and nutrients than topsoil. Some plant roots are found here.

Last is the lowest layer. It is made up of pebbles and chunks of rocks. No plant roots are found here. At the bottom is solid rock called **bedrock**.

Try It Out

Separate the Soil

- Spoon some soil into a glass jar.
- Fill the jar with water.
- Put the lid on. Then shake.
- Let the mixture settle for a few days.
- What do you see?

humus

water

rocks and sand

How Does Soil Stack Up?

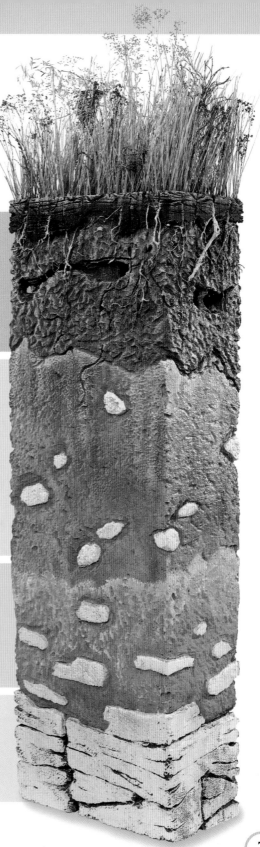

Topsoil
- fine grains
- many roots
- lots of humus

Subsoil
- not much humus
- large grains
- few roots

Lowest Layer
- no humus
- many large rocks
- no roots

Bedrock
- solid rock
- soil-making begins here

Types of Soil

There are different types of soil.
Sandy soil is made up of large grains.
Water drains through it quickly.
Clay soil is made up of tiny grains.
Water drains through it slowly.
Silt contains medium-sized grains.
Loam is a mixture of sand, clay and
silt. It is good for growing plants.

sandy soil

clay soil

silt

loam

Try It Out

Dig In!

- Collect different kinds of soil from the ground.

- Rub some soil between your fingers.

- How does it feel? Is it rough or smooth? Is it dry or wet? Does it feel like sand or clay?

- Try another sample to compare.

Crops such as lettuce grow well in loam.

Different soils suit different plants.
Loam is the best soil for farming.
It contains many **nutrients** and
holds water.

Clay soil has many nutrients too.
Yet, many plants do not grow well
in it. Plant roots cannot push through
clay soil to find water.

Sandy soil does not hold enough
water or nutrients for many plants
to grow.

Few plants can grow in the
sandy soil in Jordan.

Animals in the Soil

wombat

mole

Moles dig long
tunnels under fields
and gardens.

Soil is home for animals as well
as plants. It provides them with
food, warmth and protection.
Wombats, moles, badgers and
rabbits, dig under the soil to
make their homes, or **burrows**.
They keep the animals safe
and warm. Earthworms and
insects live in the soil, too.
They eat decaying plants.

badger

Animals help the soil by living in it. As worms and insects move through the soil, they mix the layers. Water and air can also pass through burrows to reach plants' roots. Air and water can also help to break down underground rocks to make more soil.

Animals that eat plants also help when they digest this food. They pass some of the **nutrients** from the food back into the soil in the form of waste. When these animals die, their remains **decay** and become **humus**.

Earthworms: Soil's Best Helpers

Earthworms are very important soil animals. They help by:

- Eating decaying plants, which helps break them down

- Making tunnels that let water and air into the soil

- Mixing up the soil layers

earthworm

Soils and Farming

Keeping soil healthy has always been important to farmers. That's because it can take thousands of years to form enough good soil for farming. Farmers need to protect the soil they have.

For years, farmers spread animal waste on their land to return **nutrients** to the soil. Then, as farms grew larger, some farmers began to use chemical fertilizers to enrich the soil. They began to use other chemicals to kill insects that ate crops, too.

A small plane sprays
chemicals onto a field.

Aphids are a ladybird's favourite food.

aphids

ladybird

Now farmers know that some chemicals can harm the soil. They are trying to find safer ways to protect their crops. Some farmers use ladybirds to control pests. Ladybirds eat other insects, but not plants. One ladybird can eat as many as 5,000 insects in its lifetime.

Farmers have found ways to stop soil **erosion**. They change the crops they grow each year and they plant trees to block the wind. They plough in rows around hills instead of straight up and down.

Ploughing around hills in steps helps stop soil erosion in Bali, Indonesia.

Taking Care of Soil

Now that you know why soil is important, you may want to help take care of it. People can help the soil by adding compost to it. Compost is a mixture of dry things, like dried leaves and grass, and moist things, such as fruit and vegetable scraps. When these things are combined and allowed to **decay**, they become **humus**. Compost helps the soil, and that helps the Earth.

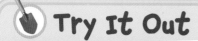
Try It Out

Make Your Own Humus

- Collect dried leaves, hedge clippings and grass cuttings.

- Gather the same amount of fruit, vegetable and ground coffee scraps.

- Combine them in a special pile outdoors. This mixture is called compost. In six to eight weeks, it will decay and become humus.

Glossary

bacteria	microscopic animal life
bedrock	the bottom layer of soil where soil-making begins
burrows	holes or tunnels dug by animals
clay	soil made from tiny grains of rock
decay	to break down slowly
erosion	wearing away of rock or soil
fungi	substances like mould, yeast, mushrooms and toadstools
humus	bits of decaying plants and animals in soil
loam	a mixture of clay, silt and sand
nutrients	materials that plants and animals need to live and grow; food
pollute	to add harmful substances
silt	soil made from medium-sized grains
subsoil	the layer of soil below the topsoil
topsoil	the top layer of soil
weathering	breaking down of rocks

Index